T0417728

by Kirsty Holmes

BEARPORT
PUBLISHING

Minneapolis, Minnesota

Credits

Images are courtesy of Shutterstock.com. With thanks to GettyImages, ThinkstockPhoto, and iStockphoto. Recurring images – gravity_point, inspiring. team, Gaidamashchuk, Zakharchenko Anna. Cover – Inspiring, Amahce, Asier Romero, DashaKos, nalin chanthorn, svtdesign, Vertes Edmond Mihai, Zhe Vasylieva, graphixmania. 2–3 – Tartila, Sudowoodo, Szasz-Fabian Jozsef. 4–5 – Monkey Business Images, Rawpixel.com, svtdesign, Hung Chung Chih. 6–7 – Ground Picture, xavier gallego morell, Tartila, Goldsithney, Roman Samborskyi. 8–9 – RavenaJuly, Monkey Business Images, JJava Designs, Nadiinko, Golden Sikorka, yusufdemirci, world of vector, Ysami, Maria Korikova, cosmaa, pikepicture. 10–11 – Szasz-Fabian Jozsef, Monkey Business Images, Rawpixel.com, wavebreakmedia, Leila Divine, adecvatman, Danielala, Tartila. 12–13 – ViDI Studio, South House Studio, fizkes, Prostock-studio, Slladkaya, Roman Samborskyi, Veja, Monkey Business Images. 14–15 – ViDI Studio, Helga Khorimarko. 16–17 – Macrovector, Bernardo Emanuell, Frame Stock Footage, ViDI Studio. 18–19 – Roquillo Tebar, Roman Samborskyi, Macrovector, IKO-studio, ViDI Studio, adecvatman. 20–21 – Eric Isselee, Anton Vierietin, SpeedKingz, fizkes, Taras Grebinets, ViDI Studio, Tartila. 22–23 – Rawpixel.com, fizkes, Monkey Business Images, Daisy Daisy, Iconic Bestiary, svtdesign. 24–25 – Roman Samborskyi, Khosro, Prostock-studio, NaMong Productions92, Master1305, Cherry-Merry, Blan-k, Guppic the duck, SurfsUp, DStarky. 26–27 – Marcel Mooij, ViDI Studio, Elena Chevalier, Monkey Business Images, Sudowoodo, Sam iSam Miller, Quang Vinh Tran, SurfsUp, DStarky. 28–29 – JackF/Adobe Stock, f.t.Photographer, Monkey Business Images, wavebreakmedia, Amahce, Blan-k, Giuseppe_R, Sudowoodo, Fadri apriliyandi, Maria Korikova, FARBAI. 30 – lemono, Marish.

Library of Congress Cataloging-in-Publication Data is available at www.loc.gov or upon request from the publisher.

ISBN: 979-8-88916-462-3 (hardcover)
ISBN: 979-8-88916-467-8 (paperback)
ISBN: 979-8-88916-471-5 (ebook)

© 2024 BookLife Publishing
This edition is published by arrangement with BookLife Publishing.

For more information, write to Bearport Publishing, 5357 Penn Avenue South, Minneapolis, MN 55419.

CONTENTS

HEALTHY LIVING

WHAT IS A LIFESTYLE?

Your **lifestyle** is the way that you live your life. The things you do each day, from the foods you eat to your favorite activities, are all a part of your lifestyle.

EVERY**ONE**'S LIFESTYLE IS DIFFERENT.

WHAT IS HEALTHY LIVING?

Healthy living is a balance of looking after the body, caring for the mind, and creating strong and meaningful **relationships** with others. It might include getting plenty of sleep or reading a book. A healthy lifestyle allows you to live well.

A HEALTHY MIND

Taking care of your body and mind is important. You can look after your **physical** and **mental** health in many ways. Having healthy relationships, taking time to relax, and doing things you enjoy are great ways to keep your mind happy.

> BUILD A LIFESTYLE THAT WORKS BEST FOR YOU.

COMPUTER GAME

SCHOOL

TOY STORE

FUTURE

AMUSEMENT

PLAYGROUND

MAKING HEALTHY CHOICES

Your lifestyle is made up of many choices. How do you stay active? What kinds of foods do you eat? You don't need to make the perfect choices every time in order to have a healthy lifestyle. However, it is important to understand how different choices might make you feel.

WHAT IS WELL-BEING?

HOW DO YOU FEEL?

Feeling good about yourself and how your life is going means you are in a state of well-being. This doesn't mean you won't have any difficulties ahead. You might face some challenges, but you feel like things will be okay.

HAVING A STATE OF WELL-BEING MAKES YOU FEEL LIKE YOU CAN HANDLE ANYTHING.

EMOTIONAL WELL-BEING

Your moods, thoughts, and feelings can affect how you think and act. A good emotional well-being doesn't mean feeling happy all the time. It means feeling safe, supported, and respected by others.

SOCIAL **WELL**-BEING

Friends and family can have a big effect on your well-being. Having positive and healthy relationships with others is an important part of social well-being.

PHYSICAL WELL-BEING

Feeling sick or in pain may make you feel out of balance. Making healthy choices, taking care of your body, and asking for help when you need it are all part of looking after your physical well-being.

WHAT IS YOUR FAVORITE WAY TO MOVE YOUR BODY?

7

WHAT IS SELF-CARE?

LOOK AFTER YOURSELF

What does the word *self-care* make you think of? Self-care is anything you do to look after your well-being. That might include taking a bubble bath or going for a walk. The choice is yours!

WHAT THINGS DO YOU ENJOY DOING MOST?

SELF-CARE IS FOR YOU!

You are unique, so the things you need to do to take care of yourself are unique, too. What helps you relax? Some people enjoy solving jigsaw puzzles, while others like playing video games.

8

EATING YOUR FAVORITE FOODS

GARDENING

DRAWING

WRITING

SELF-CARE

There are many ways you can look after yourself. Find out what works best for you!

READING A BOOK

LISTENING TO MUSIC

SEEING FRIENDS

PLAYING GAMES

WATCHING A MOVIE

PLAYING SPORTS

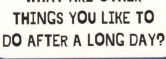

WHAT ARE OTHER THINGS YOU LIKE TO DO AFTER A LONG DAY?

MIND AND BODY

ALL ABOUT BALANCE

How you feel in your body affects your mind. Sometimes, you might **focus** on one part of your well-being and forget about another. This may tip you out of balance.

Balance is important. Worrying too much about something can make your body sick. Going a long time without seeing your loved ones can make you feel lonely. That is why balance is important for healthy living.

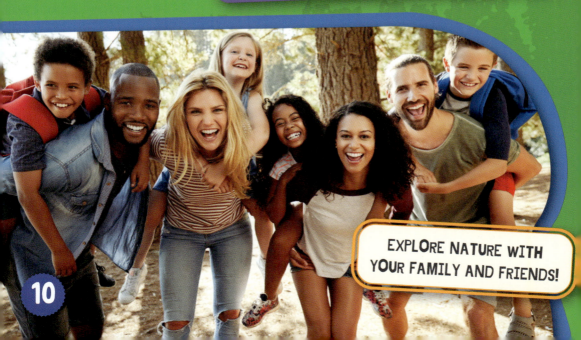

EXPLORE NATURE WITH YOUR FAMILY AND FRIENDS!

BALANCE **IN YOUR** BODY

Looking after your body is an important part of maintaining balance. Create a **diet** with the **nutrients** you need. This keeps your body working at its best. Exercising regularly will help your body and mind feel good.

YOU CAN'T ALWAYS CONTROL WHEN YOUR BODY GETS INJURED OR SICK. IT HAPPENS TO EVERYONE.

Your well-being depends on balance. A healthy body, healthy feelings, and healthy relationships are all important. Sleeping well, eating the right kind of foods, playing, and resting when you need to helps build a healthy, balanced lifestyle.

EMOTIONS

WHAT ARE EMOTIONS?

When something happens to or around you, your body reacts with emotions. We have a lot of different emotions for different situations.

SADNESS

ANGER

HAPPINESS

FEAR

DISGUST

SURPRISE

Emotions tell your body how to react to the things around you. You might want to run away when you're scared or dance if you're happy.

EMOTIONS CAN FEEL **OVERWHELMING.** SOMETIMES, YOU CAN FEEL A MIXTURE OF THEM ALL AT ONCE!

IMPORTANT EMOTIONS

Some emotions are more comfortable than others. Many people like feeling happy rather than feeling sad. But there are no good or bad emotions. Feeling all kinds of emotions is important and part of being human.

EMOTIONS CAN TELL YOU WHEN SOMETHING IS WRONG.

How people around you feel can affect your emotions, too. When your friend is happy, you might feel happy. But what if someone is angry and argues with you? This might make you upset.

UNDERSTANDING HOW PEOPLE AROUND YOU ARE FEELING IS CALLED EMPATHY.

COMPLEX EMOTIONS

MIXED EMOTIONS

Our emotions aren't always easy to understand. Sometimes, you might feel more complicated emotions than just simply anger or happiness. What if you feel both? These types of feelings are called complex emotions.

Complex emotions are a mix of two or more emotions. Let's say you feel happy and surprised. If you mix these two emotions together, you might feel excited. Complex emotions help you describe your feelings in a more **precise** way.

EMBARRASSMENT

EXCITEMENT

ANXIETY

PLAYFULNESS

LOVE

SHYNESS

FRUSTRATION

AMUSEMENT

CURIOSITY

THE LIMBIC SYSTEM

Emotions start in your brain before you feel them in your body. Different parts of the brain control different emotions and responses. Together, these parts are known as the limbic **system**.

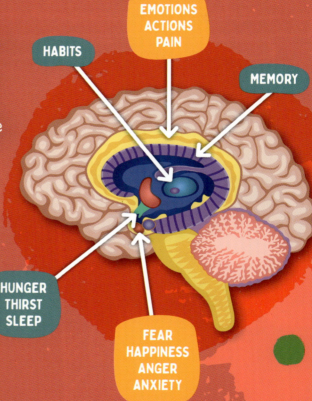

HABITS

EMOTIONS ACTIONS PAIN

MEMORY

HUNGER THIRST SLEEP

FEAR HAPPINESS ANGER ANXIETY

The limbic system works together to help you feel and respond to your emotions. When something happens to you, your limbic system works out how you should feel about it.

REACTIONS

Let's say someone you love asks for a hug. The limbic system processes this information, then sends signals to the body to respond. Your limbic system may remember the last time you hugged that person and how happy it made you feel.

What if someone pushes you instead? Your emotions warn you about danger, so you will feel a mix of fear and anger. Your body might respond with **aggression**, and you may push that person back, even if you normally wouldn't push.

YOUR LIMBIC SYSTEM RESPONDS FASTER THAN YOU CAN EVEN THINK ABOUT IT.

FEELING YOUR FEELINGS

ALL **THE** FEELS

Emotions don't just happen in the brain. Different emotions make the body do different things. When you feel angry, your heart might beat faster. If you are sad, you may feel tears in your eyes. Feeling happy can make you smile.

Your body's response to emotions can help you protect yourself. For example, when you're scared, your body may get ready to fight. Your clenched fists, tight muscles, and a beating heart might make you feel strong and powerful. Whatever has made you scared, your limbic system makes sure you are ready for it!

THINK ABOUT YOUR OTHER EMOTIONS. WHERE DO YOU FEEL THEM IN YOUR BODY?

EXPRESS YOURSELF

There are many ways to express your emotions. You can show them on your face, in your body, or in the way you act. Smiling, crying, turning red, or wrinkling your forehead are all different ways your body shows emotions.

Showing and expressing your feelings is normal. It's important not to ignore or squash them away. Find ways to express your feelings through healthy behaviors.

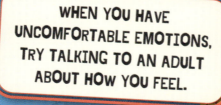

WHEN YOU HAVE UNCOMFORTABLE EMOTIONS, TRY TALKING TO AN ADULT ABOUT HOW YOU FEEL.

19

EMOTIONAL WELL-BEING

😔 **UNDERSTANDING YOUR EMOTIONS**

Sometimes, emotions can make you react without thinking. Thousands of years ago, this might have been useful for hunting. If a tiger appeared out of nowhere, it would be helpful to have the **instinct** to run away because you were scared!

Although instincts helped us in the past, having big, sudden reactions to emotions today might not be as helpful. They might make you do or say something you don't mean. It's important to try and think before we react.

REACTING TOO QUICKLY MAY CAUSE YOU TO HURT OTHERS OR EVEN YOURSELF.

MANAGING YOUR EMOTIONS

Strong emotions can be hard to manage. Naming these emotions makes it easier for you to ask for help dealing with them. Ask an adult, such as a parent or teacher, to help you express your feelings in a healthy way.

LOOKING AFTER YOUR EMOTIONAL WELL-BEING MEANS UNDERSTANDING YOUR EMOTIONS.

There are lots of ways to manage your emotions. Practice thinking about your emotions, naming them, and understanding them. Have you tried any of these?

- Writing a journal
- Talking to a friend
- Doing breathing exercises

BREATHING SLOWLY TELLS YOUR BODY YOU ARE SAFE, CALM, AND IN CONTROL.

SOCIAL WELL-BEING

HEALTHY RELATIONSHIPS

Your well-being can be affected by others, too. Connections with those around you are called relationships. They can have a positive or negative impact.

DIFFERENT TYPES OF RELATIONSHIPS MAY FORM IN DIFFERENT WAYS.

You might have relationships with your parents, friends, siblings, classmates, and teachers. Because relationships form with many different kinds of people, each one is unique. It is healthy to have many different relationships in your life.

UPS . . .

Healthy relationships are built on shared **values**. These include:

- Trust
- Honesty
- Respect
- Reliability
- Kindness

Someone who is in a healthy relationship with you will have your best interests at heart. These relationships will make you feel good about yourself and your life.

IN A HEALTHY RELATIONSHIP, BOTH PEOPLE ARE EQUALLY IMPORTANT.

. . . AND DOWNS

If a relationship is not built on shared values, it can become unhealthy. When one person's needs become more important than the other's, things get unbalanced. This sort of relationship can cause problems with your well-being.

IF SOMEONE IS NOT TREATING YOU WITH KINDNESS, THEY ARE NOT YOUR FRIEND. ASK AN ADULT YOU TRUST FOR HELP.

IT'S GOOD TO BE ME

SELF-ESTEEM

The most important person who controls your well-being is you! How you feel about yourself is called self-esteem. High self-esteem means feeling good about many different parts of your life.

- Things you can do
- Facing new challenges
- Who you are
- How others see you

CONFIDENT

STRONG

CREATIVE

KIND

PROUD

CAN I DO IT?

AM I GOOD ENOUGH?

I ALWAYS GET THE ANSWERS WRONG.

If you have low self-esteem, you might focus on mistakes, challenges, or problems. You might not feel ready to deal with the things life throws at you. What if you aren't good enough? Is self-care even worth it?

KNOW YOURSELF

The little things you like, do, think, and feel make up who you are. There is no right or wrong way to be. Knowing who you are helps you focus on having high self-esteem.

KIND TO ANIMALS

PLAYS VIOLIN

LOVES SCIENCE

FUNNY

GREAT AT FOOTBALL

LOVES SHARKS

LOYAL FRIEND

ENERGETIC

Write a list of all the positive things you can say about yourself. These could be your skills, likes, thoughts, feelings, beliefs, and actions. All the things on this list are what makes you who you are.

WHENEVER YOU HAVE A MOMENT OF SELF-DOUBT, COME BACK TO THIS LIST!

25

SLEEP

GET **YOUR** SNOOZES IN

Sleep helps your body and mind recover the energy it used throughout the day. This is important because you are growing, developing, and learning all the time.

MOST YOUNG PEOPLE NEED BETWEEN 9 AND 12 HOURS OF SLEEP EVERY NIGHT.

IT'S BEST TO REST

Not getting enough sleep can affect your well-being. Feeling tired, **anxious**, or grumpy can all be signs that you need some sleep. Even one sleepless night can cause problems.

FALLING ASLEEP DURING THE DAY MIGHT MEAN YOU NEED MORE SLEEP AT NIGHT.

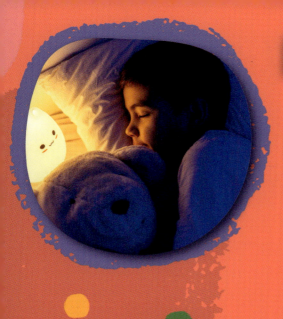

FEELING SLEEPY?

Having a bedtime routine can help tell your body it is time to sleep. What might you do for your routine?

- Putting on pajamas
- Reading a story
- Taking a shower
- Brushing your teeth

MY BEDTIME ROUTINE

Everyone's bedtime routine is different, but it should include things that help you feel relaxed, calm, and sleepy. You might meditate or write in a journal. What does your bedtime routine look like?

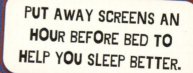

PUT AWAY SCREENS AN HOUR BEFORE BED TO HELP YOU SLEEP BETTER.

LOOK AFTER YOUR WELL-BEING

ME TIME

Me time means taking time for yourself. No matter how busy life gets, it's important to have time that's all about you. Read a book or play a video game. What are your favorite hobbies? Use this time to do anything that you like to do.

ME AND YOU TIME

Keeping in touch with your loved ones helps your well-being, too. Try walking outside, watching a movie, or having lunch together. If you can't meet up with them in person, make a video call or send them a text.

WHEN YOU HAVE SOMEONE TO RELY ON, IT'S EASIER FOR YOU TO TAKE RISKS AND GROW.

STRETCH **IT OUT**

Stretch out your tight or tired muscles. This helps you release any **tension** from your day. Practicing yoga is one great way to stretch. This exercise also helps you focus on breathing.

RELAXING THE BODY CAN HELP RELAX THE MIND AND CALM YOUR THOUGHTS.

RELAX **YOUR MIND**

When the mind is busy, meditation can help get it under control. Meditation uses breathing, stillness, and quiet to help you focus your thoughts. Find somewhere comfortable to sit. Then, focus on breathing in and out slowly.

EMPTY YOUR THOUGHTS OR FOCUS ON ONE SPECIFIC THING AS YOU MEDITATE.

Affirmations

Affirmations are positive statements that you say to yourself. Look into a mirror and say them out loud. Practicing affirmations every day can help your emotional well-being. Let's give some a try. Say it like you mean it!

I BELIEVE IN MYSELF.

I LOVE MYSELF BECAUSE . . .

MY FEELINGS MATTER.

I CAN LEARN FROM MY MISTAKES.

I AM PROUD OF MYSELF.

No matter how you do it, taking care of your body, emotions, and relationships helps you live well. Are you ready to find balance?

GLOSSARY

aggression threatening or angry behavior directed at another person

anxious worried

diet the food that a person usually eats

focus to pay attention to something

instinct something a person does naturally, without having to learn it

lifestyle a way of living that reflects the things a person finds important

mental having to do with the mind

nutrients proteins, vitamins, fats, and other things in food that are needed to stay healthy

overwhelming tending to make one feel overpowered by too much at once

physical relating to the body

precise something that is exact or very accurate

relationships the connections that people have with one another

system a group of parts working together to achieve a job or goal

tension strain or tightness in the muscles

values a person's beliefs and ideas about what is important

INDEX

READ MORE

Kukla, Lauren. *Breathe with Art! Activities to Manage Emotions (Wellness Workshop).* Minneapolis: Abdo Publishing, 2023.

Markovics, Joyce L. *Emotions (Mind Blowing! The Brain).* Ann Arbor, MI: Cherry Lake Publishing, 2023.

LEARN MORE ONLINE

1. Go to **www.factsurfer.com** or scan the QR code below.

2. Enter "**Healthy Mind**" into the search box.

3. Click on the cover of this book to see a list of websites.